彩虹的颜色
Rainbow Colors

美国迪士尼公司 编著
（美）莎拉·海尔·米勒 改编
黄如露 翻译

外语教学与研究出版社
FOREIGN LANGUAGE TEACHING AND RESEARCH PRESS
北京 BEIJING

一天，跳跳虎和小豆在小熊维尼家里画画。

维尼透过窗户，看到雨已经停了。他说："我们出去玩吧。"

Pooh looks out the **window**. It's not **rainy** now! He says, "Let's go out and play."

window	窗户
rainy	下雨的
happy	高兴的
want	想要

"同意！"跳跳虎和小豆高兴地说。他们再也不想继续呆在屋里了。

Tigger and Roo are **happy**. They don't **want** to play inside anymore.

于是，小豆、维尼和跳跳虎一起朝小河边走去。下过雨之后，树叶和花朵看起来美极了！瑞比和屹耳已经在河边玩耍了！

They **walk** to the river. Rabbit and Eeyore are there.

walk	走
hi	你（们）好
you	你（们）
play a game	做游戏
yes	是的

"你们好！"小豆说，"你们想一起做游戏吗？"

"当然了！"瑞比答道，"我们玩什么呢？"

Roo says, "**Hi**, guys! Do **you** want to **play a game**?"
Rabbit says, "Oh, **yes**! What can we play?"

原来是扔木棍游戏。小伙伴们捡好木棍之后，在桥上站好。

"一、二、三！"瑞比喊完之后，大家一起把木棍用力向水里扔去。木棍顺着水流漂到小桥下面。

The **friends stand** on the bridge. They throw sticks in the **water**.

谁的木棍会最先出现在小桥的另一边呢?

"看!我的木棍第一!"小豆兴奋地喊道。

Whose stick will be the first to show up?
Roo says, "Look! **Mine** is the first!"

friends	朋友,friend的复数形式
stand	站立
water	水
mine	我的(东西)

突然，维尼指着小河喊道："看！那是什么？"

"哇，好漂亮的颜色啊！"瑞比惊叹道。

Pooh says, "Look! What's that?"
Rabbit says, "Wow, such **pretty colors**!"

小豆和跳跳虎开心地跳起舞来。

他们一边跳,一边唱:"那是彩虹,漂亮的彩虹!"

Roo and Tigger start to **dance**.
They **sing**, "It's a rainbow, a rainbow!"

pretty	漂亮的
colors	颜色,color的复数形式
dance	跳舞
sing	唱歌

就在这时,猫头鹰朝大家飞来。

"嘿,猫头鹰!"跳跳虎喊道,"快看你的身后,有彩虹!"

Owl **flies down** to the friends.
Tigger shouts, "Owl, look at the rainbow!"

flies	飞，fly的第三人称单数形式
down	朝下
sad	难过的

可是等猫头鹰转身看的时候，已经太迟了，彩虹消失了。

"噢，我错过了彩虹。"猫头鹰说，"这太可惜了。"接着就沮丧地飞走了。

Owl turns around, but he's too late.

"Oh, I missed it," he says. He's **sad**. He flies away.

伙伴们也为他感到难过。怎样才能让猫头鹰高兴起来呢？

"嘿，伙计们！"跳跳虎说，"我们去给猫头鹰找一些彩虹的颜色吧！"

The friends are sad too. How can they make Owl happy again? Tigger says, "Let's **get** some rainbow colors for Owl!"

于是，大家分头行动，在周围寻找彩虹的颜色。他们发现百亩林里有各种各样的颜色！

They look around. They **find** colors everywhere!

get	去拿
find	发现

突然，一阵大风吹来，小豆发现一些红色的东西在空中飞舞。

"红色！"小豆一边喊，一边飞快地朝那些红色的羽毛追去。

It's **windy**. **Something red** dances in the air.
Roo shouts, "Red!" He **runs** after the feathers.

维尼看见一只蚱蜢从身边跳过,连忙跟了上去。蚱蜢带着他来到了一片草地上。维尼抬头一看,发现眼前都是绿色的三叶草!有的居然长着四片叶子!

Pooh follows a grasshopper.
Wow! He sees **green** clovers everywhere!

wIndy	风大的
something	某种东西
red	红色的
runs	跑,run的第三人称单数形式
green	绿色的

15

跳跳虎睁大眼睛，想找到橙色的东西。这是什么？

Tigger **opens** his **eyes** wide.
What's this?

opens	睁开，open的第三人称单数形式
eyes	眼睛，eye的复数形式
orange	橙色的
flowers	花，flower的复数形式

跳跳虎低头一看，原来在他跳来跳去的地方就长着一些橙色的小花！

跳跳虎高兴极了，"这些花的颜色和我一样！"

Orange flowers are everywhere!

Tigger is happy. "These flowers are in the same color as me!" he says.

屹耳想找蓝色的东西，但是他肚子饿了，决定先找点儿吃的。他在灌木丛中找到了一些蓝莓，发现它们正是蓝色的！

Eeyore is hungry. He looks for something to **eat**. He sees something **blue**—blueberries!

eat	吃
blue	蓝色的
tall	高的
one	一
yellow	黄色的

此时，瑞比正在努力寻找黄色的东西。他看见几株长得很高的植物，就从上面摘了一个果实下来。剥掉外面的苞叶，黄灿灿的玉米就露了出来！

Rabbit sees some **tall** plants.
He opens **one**. He sees something **yellow** inside! It's yellow corn.

大家把找到的各种颜色的东西都放在一起。

"现在，我们可以给猫头鹰制作一道彩虹了。"维尼说。

屹耳说："我们没有紫色的东西。"

Pooh says, "We **have** a rainbow for Owl now!"

Eeyore says, "We don't have something **purple**."

have	有
purple	紫色的

就在大家垂头丧气地想办法时,小猪拎着篮子跑了过来。

"等一等!"小猪喊道,"我找到了一些紫色的小花!"

"Wait!" Piglet says. "Here are some purple flowers!"

小伙伴们把各种颜色的东西整齐地摆放在草地上。
The friends **put** everything together.

put	放置
there are...	有……

红色的羽毛、橙色的花朵、黄色的玉米、绿色的三叶草、蓝色的浆果和紫色的牵牛花……组成了一道美丽的彩虹!

There are red feathers, orange flowers, yellow corn, green clovers, blue blueberries, and purple flowers... What a beautiful rainbow for Owl!

他们爬到猫头鹰的树屋上。

跳跳虎一边敲门，一边喊道："猫头鹰，快出来，我们把彩虹给你带来了！"

"太棒了！"猫头鹰惊讶极了，"这是我见过的最漂亮的彩虹！你们都是我最好的朋友，谢谢你们！"

They go to Owl's **house**.

Tigger says, "Owl, we have another rainbow for you!"

Owl is very surprised. "What a beautiful rainbow! And what good friends you all are!"

house	房子

维尼英语小学堂

主题词

小朋友，这些颜色你都认识吗？

red

orange

purple

yellow

blue

green

写一写

猫头鹰没有看到彩虹，感到很沮丧。百亩林里的小伙伴们决定分头去给猫头鹰找一些彩虹的颜色。他们都找到了什么颜色？请根据图片的提示，把下面的单词补充完整吧。

yello__

bl__e

oran__e

g__een

pur__le

r__d

猜一猜

袋鼠妈妈给小豆出了一道谜题,这可把小豆难住了。小朋友,你能帮帮小豆吗?想一想横线上应该填写什么字母。

提示:R=red O=orange Y=yellow G=green B=blue P=purple

P　B　P　＿　＿

＿　O　＿　＿　＿　R

请你自己设计规律,给下面的图案涂上颜色,并在下面的横线上填上合适的字母。

涂一涂

小朋友，下面的颜色单词你都认识吗？请根据单词提示，给下面的图案涂上颜色吧。

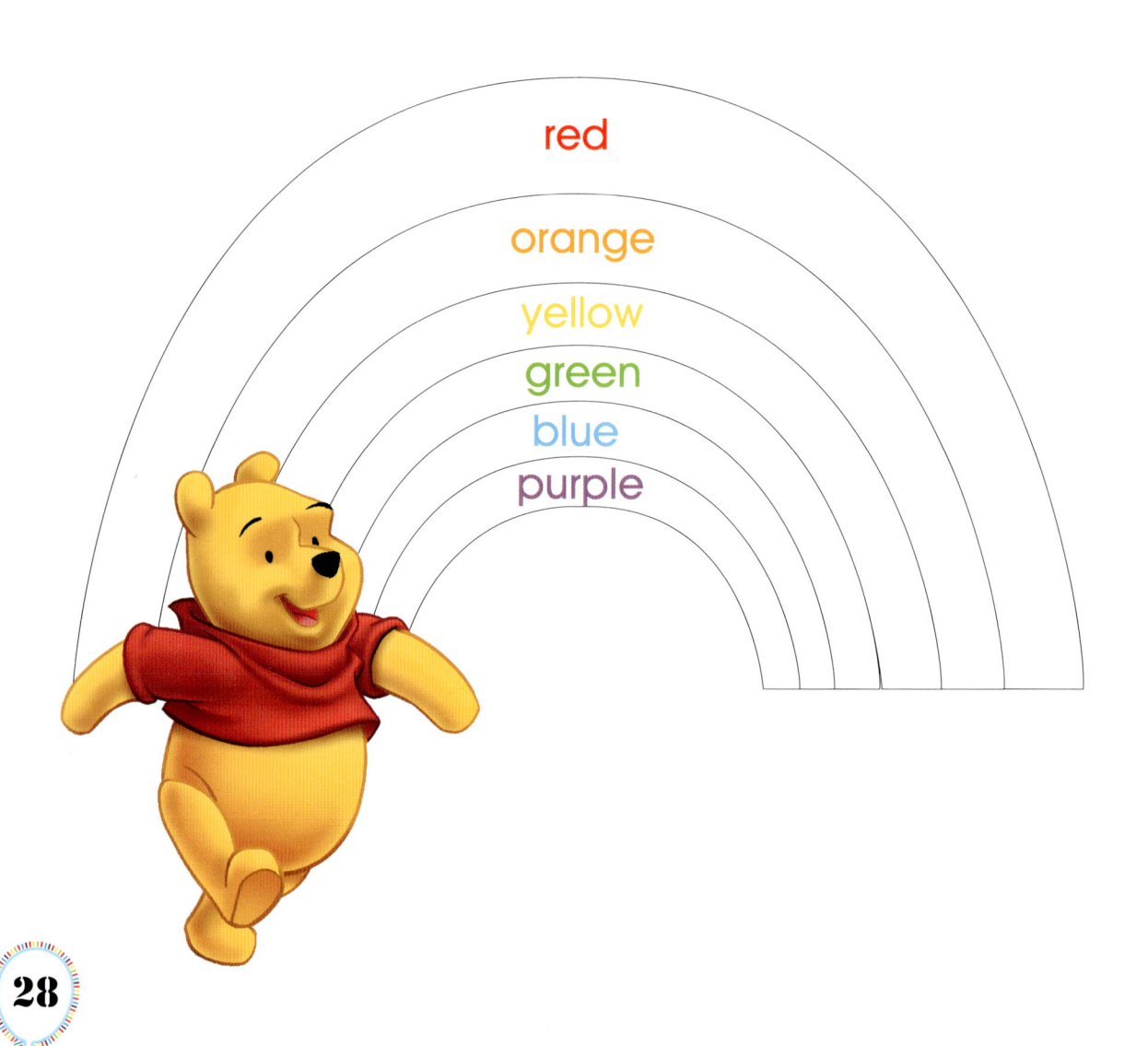

red

orange

yellow

green

blue

purple

词汇表

B
blue 蓝色的

C
colors 颜色，color的复数形式

D
dance 跳舞
down 向下

E
eat 吃
eyes 眼睛，eye的复数形式

F
find 发现
flies 飞，fly的第三人称单数形式
flowers 花，flower的复数形式

G
get 得到
green 绿色的

H
happy 高兴的
have 有
hi 你(们)好
house 房子

M
mine 我的（东西）

O
one 一
opens 打开，open的第三人称单数形式
orange 橙色的

P
play a game 做游戏
pretty 漂亮的
purple 紫色的
put 放置

R
rainy 下雨的
red 红色的
runs 跑，run的第三人称单数形式

S
sad 难过的
sing 唱歌
something 某种东西
stand 站立

T
tall 高的
there are... 有……

W
walk 走
want 想要
water 水
window 窗户
windy 风大的

Y
yellow 黄色的
yes 是的
you 你（们）

friends 朋友（们），friend的复数形式

词汇表

B
ball 球
bathroom 浴室
big 大的
blue 蓝色的

C
carrots 胡萝卜，carrot的复数形式
circle 圆形

D
diamond 菱形
down 朝下

E
eat 吃
eggs 蛋，egg的复数形式

F
flies 飞，fly的第三人称单数形式

G
green 绿色的

H
hat 帽子
have 有
heart 心形
hi 你（们）好

J
jumps 跳，jump的第三人称单数形式

K
kitchen 厨房

L
like 喜欢

M
mom 妈妈

N
nice 好的

O
oval 椭圆形

P
paper 纸质的
play a game 做游戏

R
rectangle 长方形
red 红色的

S
see 看见
shape 形状
small 小的
something 某种东西
squares 正方形，square的复数形式
sweet 甜的

T
thank you 谢谢你（们）
there are... 有……
triangle 三角形

U
up 朝上

W
want 想要

Y
yes 是的
your 你（们）的

画一画

小朋友，故事中出现的形状，你都记住了吗？请根据图片和单词提示，在右边的方框里画出相应的图形，并练习读单词。

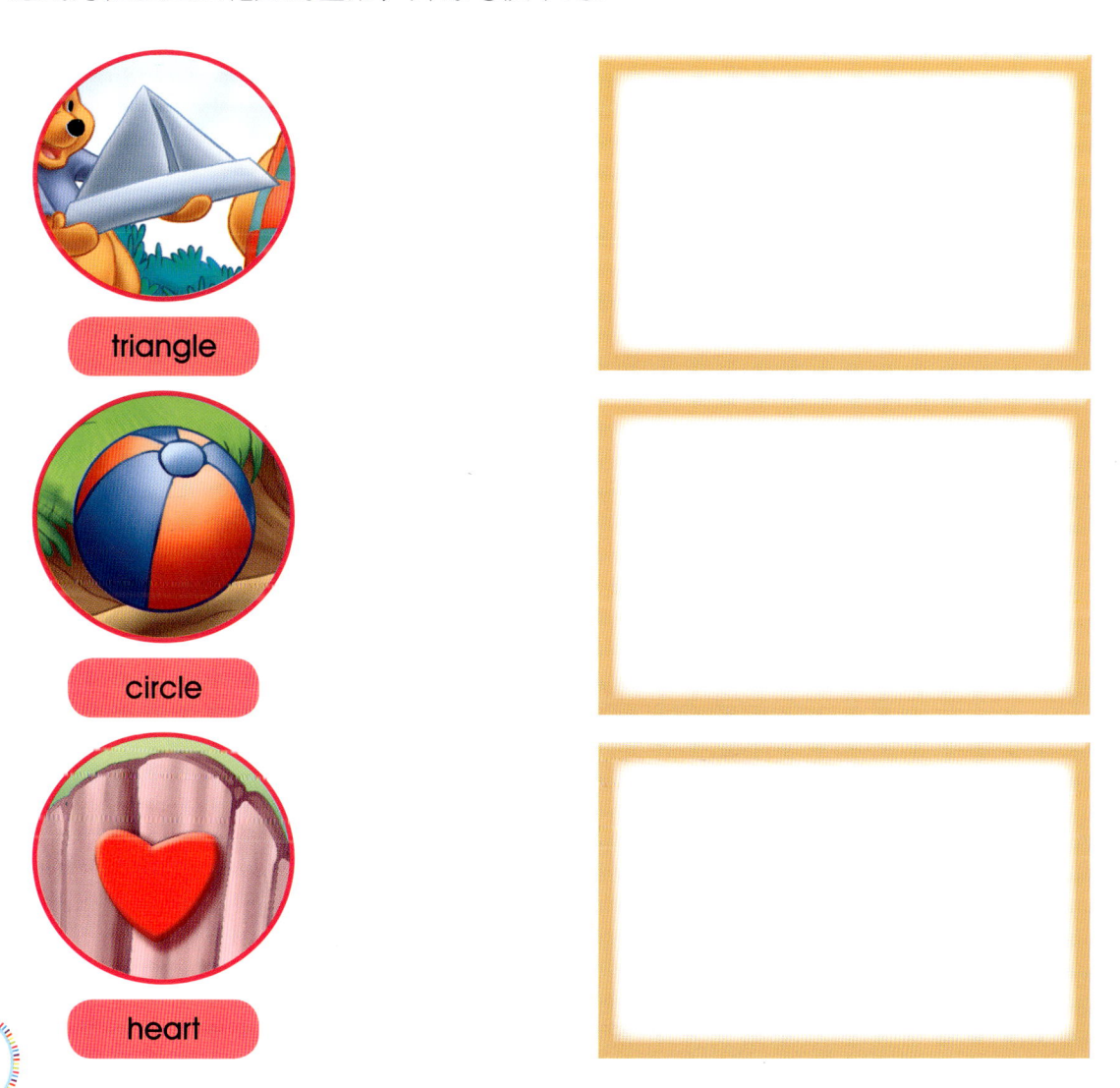

triangle

circle

heart

写一写

小豆今天很开心,因为他认识了很多形状。他想把这些形状记在日记本上,可是发现有一些单词不会拼写。请你根据小豆画的形状,在横线上写出正确的字母,帮他完成今天的日记。

tri__ngle

dia__ond

__val

re__tangle

h__art

连一连

百亩林里的小伙伴们正在玩"形状找找看"的游戏,你也一起来找一找吧。请把图片和对应的单词连起来。

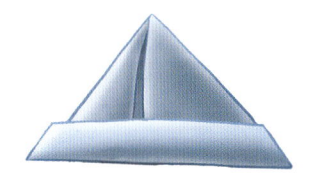

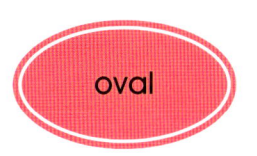

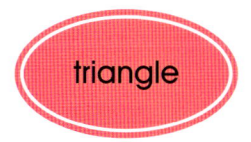

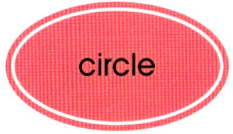

oval

triangle

circle

square

维尼英语小学堂

主题词

小朋友，这些形状你都认识吗？

heart

triangle

diamond

circle

oval

square

rectangle

"最后一题！"瑞比说，"我想到一样东西。它是圆形的，很好吃，味道很甜美！"

"是蓝莓！"小豆说，"瑞比，我们能摘一些吗？"

"当然！"瑞比回答，"这些圆形的东西十分美味！"

Rabbit has one last guessing game. "It's a circle. It's **sweet**. It's **nice** to **eat**!"

"A blueberry!" Roo says. "May we have some, Rabbit?"

"Yes!" Rabbit says. "These circles are delicious!"

sweet	甜的
nice	好的
eat	吃

袋鼠妈妈的篮子里都有什么呢？胡萝卜、土豆和西红柿！

What does she have? **Carrots**, potatoes, and tomatoes!

have	有
carrots	胡萝卜，carrot的复数形式

现在，袋鼠妈妈的篮子已经装满了新鲜的蔬菜。

"看，妈妈！"小豆说，"你的篮子里有三角形、椭圆形，还有圆形！"

Kanga's basket is full now.
Roo says, "Look, Mom! You **have** triangles, ovals, and circles in your basket!"

袋鼠妈妈说:"我想到了一个长方形。它在我们的浴室和厨房里。"

"我知道!"小豆笑着说,"是肥皂!它是长方形的。"

Kanga says, "It's a rectangle. It's in our **bathroom** and **kitchen**." Roo laughs, "It's a bar of soap!"

| bathroom | 浴室 |
| kitchen | 厨房 |

"是西瓜!"罗宾和小豆同时喊道。

"真棒!"瑞比说,"你们猜对了!"

"这个游戏太好玩儿了,妈妈!"小豆说,"谁还能找到更多的形状?"

"A watermelon!" Christopher Robin and Roo shout together.

red	红色的
heart	心形
green	绿色的

"我也有一题要考大家。"瑞比说,"我发现了一个椭圆形。它是绿色的,今天就可以采摘了。"

罗宾、袋鼠妈妈和小豆赶紧在菜园里寻找。

Rabbit says, "I spy an oval. It's **green**. It's ready to pick today."

现在轮到小豆提问了。他说:"我发现了一个红色的心形!它在哪儿呢?"

袋鼠妈妈看了看瑞比的菜园,回答道:"它在瑞比家菜园的门上!"

It's Roo's turn. "I spy a **red heart**! Where is it?"

"Hmm," Kanga says. "It's on Rabbit's gate."

"是你的气球！"小豆回答道。

Roo answers, "It's your balloon!"

big	大的
blue	蓝色的

罗宾也来到了瑞比的菜园。

"我可以和你一起做游戏吗？"他对小豆说，"我发现了一个椭圆形。它很大，是蓝色的。如果你猜对了，我就把它送给你。"

"Can I play too?" Christopher Robin says. "I spy an oval. It's **big** and **blue**. If you can guess it, I'll give it to you!"

"我知道!是我拿的这块牌子!"瑞比回答道,"上面画的胡萝卜看起来像一个三角形。"

Rabbit says, "I know! It's this sign!"

hi	你(们)好
want	想要
rectangle	长方形

这时，他们看见瑞比拿着一块牌子站在菜园里。

"你好，瑞比！"小豆说，"你想和我们一起玩'形状找找看'的游戏吗？我发现了一个长方形，它里面有一个三角形。你知道那是什么吗？"

"**Hi**, Rabbit!" Roo says. "Do you **want** to play a game with us? I spy a triangle in a **rectangle**. What is it?"

袋鼠妈妈看了看周围,"我在一个小篮子里发现了一些椭圆形的东西。"

"是什么呢?"小豆说,"是蛋!"

Kanga looks around. "I spy **something oval** in a **small** basket."
"What is it? **Eggs**!" says Roo.

up	朝上
down	朝下
something	某种东西
oval	椭圆形
small	小的
eggs	蛋,egg的复数形式

"我发现了一个正方形。"袋鼠妈妈说。

就在这时,一只小鸟飞了过来,停在瑞比家附近的一个指示牌上。

"正方形在那儿,妈妈!"小豆一蹦一跳地说,"是瑞比的菜园指示牌。"

Kanga says, "I spy a square."

Roo jumps **up** and **down**. "It's Rabbit's garden sign!"

see 看见

"在哪里呀？"小豆嘀咕道，"哦，我看见它了。是那个车轮！"

"Where's the circle?" Roo says. "Oh, I **see** it. It's that wheel!"

"真好玩儿!"小豆说,"下一个是什么?"

"让我看看……"袋鼠妈妈说,"我发现了另一个圆形。它很结实,是木头做的。"

"I spy another circle," Kanga says. "It's strong, round, and made of wood."

"你真棒，小豆！"袋鼠妈妈说，"现在来听下一个，我发现了一个菱形。它在空中飞！"

"那是屹耳的风筝！"小豆兴奋地喊道。

Kanga says, "I spy a **diamond**. It **flies** in the sky."

Roo points. "It's Eeyore's kite!"

circle	圆形
jumps	跳，jump的第三人称单数形式
ball	球
diamond	菱形
flies	飞，fly的第三人称单数形式

"这个游戏叫'形状找找看'。"袋鼠妈妈说,"我发现了一个圆形。它可以跳得很高。"

小豆看了看周围,喊道:"是球!"

Kanga says, "I spy a **circle**. It **jumps** high."
Roo shouts, "It's a **ball**!"

squares	正方形，square的复数形式
play a game	做游戏
like	喜欢

在去菜园的路上，袋鼠妈妈说："我们一起做游戏吧！我知道一个很棒的游戏。"

小豆高兴极了，"太好了，我喜欢做游戏。是什么呀？"

On the way to Rabbit's garden, Kanga says, "Let's **play a game**! I know a good game."

Roo says, "A game? I **like** games. What is it?"

"你的围裙上有很多正方形的图案！"小豆说。

"你真棒！"袋鼠妈妈说，"现在，我们去瑞比的菜园里摘一些蔬菜吧。"

Roo says, "There are **squares** on your apron!"

"Very good!" Kanga says. "Now it's time to go to Rabbit's garden for more vegetables."

"是的，你说对了！"袋鼠妈妈回答，"你的周围还有很多其他形状的东西，你能把它们找出来吗？"

"**Yes**, you're right!" Kanga says. "**There are** shapes everywhere! Look around!"

shape	形状
your	你(们)的
triangle	三角形
yes	是的
there are...	有……

"小豆，你知道你的帽子是什么形状的吗？"袋鼠妈妈问。

小豆把帽子从头上拿下来，仔细地看了看，不确定地说："它是三角形的吗？"

"What **shape** is **your** hat? Do you know?" says Kanga.
Roo says, "Is it a **triangle**?"

袋鼠妈妈给小豆做了一顶纸帽子。小豆戴着它在草地上玩耍。

"我是一个小海盗！"小豆喊道，"妈妈，谢谢你给我做了这顶帽子！"

Kanga makes Roo a **paper hat**.
Roo says, "**Thank you**, **Mom**!"

paper	纸质的
hat	帽子
thank you	谢谢你（们）
mom	妈妈

致家长朋友

"迪士尼英语家庭版"系列图书是由迪士尼英语教育专家与外语教学与研究出版社共同打造的一套高品质、兼具科学性和系统性的优秀双语儿童读物,有故事书、游戏书、词典等丰富的图书种类。

"迪士尼英语家庭版"系列图书采用中英双语"不对称对照"的形式,中文部分生动有趣,英文部分简单易懂,同时解决了孩子英语学习的意愿和能力问题。为了使孩子的英语水平在阅读中得到切实的提高,每本书都有一到两个英语学习主题,并围绕这个主题设计了好玩儿的英语小游戏。不仅如此,每本图书还都配有免费的双语音频,为孩子量身打造最适宜的双语学习环境。

"小熊维尼双语认知故事"系列将儿童认知的内容,如形状、颜色、感觉、想象力、创造力等,与双语故事相结合。孩子在阅读故事、学习英语的同时,还能够扩展知识面,提高认知能力。